Braided Creek

Jim Harrison & Ted Kooser

BRAIDED
CREEK

A Conversation in Poetry

Copper Canyon Press

Grateful acknowledgment is made to Russell Chatham for the use of *Afternoon on Sweetgrass Creek* on the cover.

Several poems from *Braided Creek* first appeared in the chapbook "A Conversation," published by Aralia Press.

Copper Canyon Press is in residence under the auspices of the Centrum Foundation at Fort Worden State Park in Port Townsend, Washington. Centrum sponsors artist residencies, education workshops for Washington State students and teachers, Blues, Jazz, and Fiddle Tunes festivals, classical music performances, and the Port Townsend Writers' Conference.

LIBRARY OF CONGRESS CATALOGING-IN-PUBLICATION DATA

Harrison, Jim, 1937–

Braided Creek: a conversation in poetry / by Jim Harrison & Ted Kooser.

  p. cm.

ISBN 1-55659-187-x (pbk. edition: alk. paper) —

ISBN 1-55659-188-8 (limited edition: alk. paper)

1. Nature — Poetry. 1. Kooser, Ted. 11. Title.

PS3558.A67B73 2003

811'.54 — DC21   2002154797

9 8 7 6 5 4 3 2 FIRST PRINTING

COPPER CANYON PRESS

Post Office Box 271, Port Townsend, Washington 98368

www.coppercanyonpress.org

To Dan Gerber

How one old tire leans up against
another, the breath gone out of both.

Old friend,
perhaps we work too hard
at being remembered.

Which way will the creek
run when time ends?
Don't ask me until
this wine bottle is empty.

While my bowl is still half full,
you can eat out of it too,
and when it is empty,
just bury it out in the flowers.

All those years
I had in my pocket.
I spent them,
nickel-and-dime.

Each clock tick falls
like a raindrop,
right through the floor
as if it were nothing.

In the morning light,
the doorknob, cold with dew.

The Pilot razor-point pen is my
compass, watch, and soul chaser.
Thousands of miles of black squiggles.

Under the storyteller's hat
are many heads, all troubled.

At dawn, a rabbit stretches tall
to eat the red asparagus berries.

The big fat garter snake
emerged from the gas-stove burner
where she had coiled around the pilot light
for warmth on a cold night.

Straining on the toilet
we learn how
the lightning bug feels.

For sixty-three years I've ground myself
within this karmic mortar. Yesterday I washed
it out and put it high on the pantry shelf.

All I want to be
is a thousand blackbirds
bursting from a tree,
seeding the sky.

Republicans think that all over the world
darker-skinned people are having more fun
than they are. It's largely true.

Faucet dripping into a pan,
dog lapping water,
the same sweet music.

The nuthatch is in business
on the tree trunk,
fortunes up and down.

Oh what dew
these mortals be.
Dawn to dark.
One long breath.

The wit of the corpse
is lost on the lid of the coffin.

A book on the arm of my chair
and the morning before me.

Everyone thought I'd die
in my twenties, thirties, forties, fifties.
This can't go on forever.

There are mornings
when everything brims with promise,
even my empty cup.

Two squirrels fight
to near death,
red blood flecking green grass,
while chipmunks continue feeding.

What pleasure: a new straw hat
with a green brim to look through!

Rowing across the lake
all the dragonflies are screwing.
Stop it. It's Sunday.

Throw out the anchor
unattached to a rope.
Heart lifts as it sinks.
Out of my mind at last.

On every topographic map,
the fingerprints of God.

When we were very poor one spring
I fished a snowy river and caught
a big trout. It changed our lives
that day: eating, drinking, singing, dancing.

Lost: Ambition.
Found: A good book,
an old sweater,
loose shoes.

Years ago
when I became tough as a nail
I became a nail.

An old song from my youth:
"I'm going to live, live, live
until I die." Well, perhaps not.

Still at times I'm a dumb little boy
fishing from a rowboat in the rain
wanting to give the family a fish dinner.

Only today
I heard
the river
within the river.

Clear summer dawn,
first sun steams moisture
redly off the cabin roof,
a cold fire. Passing raven
eyeballs it with a *quawk.*

The rabbit is born
prepared for listening,
the poet just for talk.

As a boy when desperate I'd pray with bare knees
on the cold floor. I still do,
but from the window I look like an old man.

Two buzzards
perched on a hay bale
and a third just gliding in.

I want to describe my life in hushed tones
like a TV nature program. *Dawn in the north.*
His nose stalks the air for newborn coffee.

Turtle has just one plan
at a time, and every cell
buys into it.

The biomass of ants,
their total weight on earth,
exceeds our own.
They welcome us to their world
of small homes, hard work, big women.

But the seventeen-year cicada
has only one syllable.

What prizes and awards will I get for revealing
the location of the human soul? As Nixon said,
I know how to win the war but I'm not telling.

Some days
one needs to hide
from possibility.

She climbed the green-leafed apple tree
in her green Sunday dress. Her white panties
were white as the moon above brown legs.

Is this poem a pebble,
or a raindrop coated with dust?

Each time I go outside the world
is different. This has happened
all my life.

When I found my tracks in the snow
I followed, thinking that they might
lead me back to where I was. But
they turned the wrong way and went on.

I schlump around the farm
in dirty, insulated coveralls
checking the private lives of mice.

I heard the lake cheeping
under the ice, too weak
to break through the shell.

Nothing to do.
Nowhere to go.
The moth just drowned
in the whiskey glass.
This is heaven.

Wind in the chimney
turns on its heel
without crushing the ashes.

Way out in the local wilderness
the only human tracks are mine, left foot
pigeon-toed, aimless.

Trust snow to keep a secret.

Old white soup bowl
chipped like a tooth,
one of us is always empty.

I used to have time by the ass
but now I share it in common
and it's going away.

These legs
are wearing out.
Uphill, downhill.
They'll love
their flat earth rest.

Old centipede
can't keep himself
from leaving.

My dog girlfriend Rose was lost
for three endless days and nights
during which I uncontrollably sobbed.

Fear is a swallow
in a boarded-up warehouse,
seeking a window out.

The brown stumps
of my old teeth
don't send up shoots
in spring.

In New York
on a wet
and bitter street
I heard a crow from home.

Mouse nest in the toe of my boot,
have I been gone that long?

I haven't forgotten
to look in the mirror,
I just don't
do it anymore.

When Time picks apples,
it eats them with the yellow teeth
of bees.

We flap our gums, our wattles, our
featherless wings in non-native air
to avoid being planted in earth,
watching the bellies of passing birds.

On its stand on the empty stage
the tuba with its big brass ear
enjoys the silence.

So what if women
no longer smile to see me?
I smile to see them!

Why do I behave so badly?
Just because. That's still
a good answer.

Now an outlander, once a poet in N.Y.
crisscrossing Gotham for food and drink,
the souls of Lorca and Crane a daily solstice.

Open the shoe-store door
and a bell rings:
two shoehorns on a shoelace.

Let go of the mind, the thousand blue
story fragments we tell ourselves
each day to keep the world underfoot.

How foolish the houseplant looks
as it offers its droopy leaves
like hands to be kissed.

I trace my noble ancestry back
to the first seed, the first cell
that emerged reluctantly from the void.

The crow comes from
a broken home.
She is so loud because
no one will listen.

Dog days
for me and the dogs,
afloat clockwise
in the river's eddy.

The deer hung flapping
high on the buffalo fence,
pushed by an inner wind.

The pigeon
has swallowed a fountain!
Listen!

The goofy young bald eagle
is ignored by the seagulls and ravens
as these enemies share
a barrel of fish heads and guts.

On Everest there are pink concealed
gnats that when falling
learn decisively that they can't fly.

Surely someone will help
the mourning mourning dove,
but who, but who?

Trees stay in place.
Fish spend a lifetime underwater.
Our last track is a skull.

A coffin handle
leaves a lasting impression
on a hand.

Oh the dark, rank, brackish rut
of money. The news from the inside
is fine. Outside, a sucking cold vacuum.

A nephew rubs the sore feet
of his aunt,
and the rope that lifts us all toward grace
creaks in the pulley.

The cups of the tulips
tip forward, spilling their snow.

Sometimes my big front teeth bite
my lower lip and my food gets bloody.
What is this argument all about?

"Do you feel your age?" she asked,
so I squeezed my age till it hurt,
then set it free.

Rising from a cramped position
before the fireplace I discover
that there's blood in my legs.

So much to live for.
Each rope rings
a different bell.

Fifty-two degrees at noon, July 2.
At the senior citizens' carwash
all the oldsters try to look vigorous.

The mirror, backed in black,
and grief behind each face.

When you drink from dawn's light
you see the bottom of the cup.

I am wherever I find myself to be,
of all places. At 6 A.M. the Paris lights
shine through the cool November rain.
Only a few hours ago there was a moon.

My new trifocals hurt my nose.
All that lifting them up and down
just to find my way.

The fat snake's gone this year.
She's been transplanted to a place
she won't hear my startled yelp
when she emerges from the stove top.

Winter knows
when a man's pockets
are empty.

Old willow
taps the river
with his cane.

I was paralyzed from the waist up
for three months. My feet walked me.
The birds all turned brown. I fell
out of a tree I hadn't climbed.

An empty boat
will volunteer for anything.

When the dollhouse was built in a month's work
a red ghost was trapped in a tiny closet.
You can hear its breathing a thousand miles.

Gentle readers, tomorrow I undergo
radical brain surgery, but don't worry.
Win some. Lose some. Mostly ties.

Wanted: Looking for owl roosts
for pellets for Science project.
Call Marli.

In each of my cells Dad and Mom
are still doing their jobs. As always,
Dad says *yes*, Mom *no*. I split the difference
and feel deep sympathy for my children.

At the tip of memory's
great funnel-cloud
is the nib of a pen.

At my cabin
to write a poem
is to throw an egg across
the narrow river into the trees.

A dozen dead houseflies,
bits of green glass from the bottle
of summer, smashed on the sill.

Getting older I'm much better at watching
rain. I skip counting individual drops
in favor of the general feeling of rain.

Like a fist, the toad
knocks on the dirt road
wanting in.

Strange world indeed:
a poet keeping himself awake
to write about insomnia.

The sparrow is not busy,
but hungry.

I remember being a cellular oyster
in a tiny geode before being prodded
into a world of lilacs and blood.

Next to a gravestone,
a green tin cup
brimful of shadows.
Must we drink?

There is just one of us.
Already you are what you are.
Old rooster crowing with a stretched neck.

I might have been a welder,
kneeling at a fountain of sparks
in my mask of stars.

The moon put her white hands
on my shoulders, looked into my face,
and without a word
sent me on into the night.

Coming home late from the tavern.
A mouse has drowned in the toilet.
A metaphor of the poet, I think.
But no, the death of a glorious mouse.

The drunken man
spills most of his importance
on his shoes.

After carefully listing my 10,000 illusions
I noticed that nearly all that I found
in the depths was lost in the shallows.

Raindrops on your glasses;
there you go again,
reading the clouds.

Dewdrops are the dreams
of the grass. They linger, shining,
into the morning.

If you can awaken
inside the familiar
and discover it strange
you need never leave home.

The birds,
confused by rain clouds,
think it's evening.

Another spring,
and a long trail of grease ants
over the breadboard.

The girl with blue shorts and brown legs
the color of the dog beside her
ran through the green orchard
kicking her butt with her own heels.

Lost for a while,
I found her name
when I scratched through
my hair.

To prevent leakage,
immerse yourself in clouds and birds,
a jubilant drift downward.

With her brush, the artist
touches one part of her life
with another.

You told me you couldn't see
a better day coming,
so I gave you my eyes.

How can Lorca say he's only the pulse
of a wound that probes to the opposite side?
I'm wondering if he ever rowed a boat backwards.

The black sleeve falls back
from the scalded fist:
a turkey vulture.

At 62 I've outlived 95 percent
of the world. I'll be home
just before dark.

All my life
I've been in the caboose
with blind glands
running the locomotive.

Letters from beautiful women.
What do they tell me?

Woodpecker,
why so much effort
for such little gain?

In Mexico the big, lovely
woman took off her blue outfit
becoming a normal woman
only more so.

The way a springer spaniel
hops through deep grass,
I was once a lover like that.

When she left me
I stood out in the thunderstorm,
hoping to be destroyed by lightning.
It missed, first left, then right.

When a hammer sings
its head is loose.

Actresses I've known grow younger
while I don't, but after my Vietnam head
wounds, I won three Olympic gold medals.

The one-eyed man must be fearful
of being taken for a birdhouse.

As a child I loved to square-dance,
a junior beast sniffing my fingers
after it touched a new girl's hand.

Reading poetry late at night
to try to come back to life.
Almost but not quite.

Now it's the body's dog, pain,
barking and barking.
A stranger has come to the gate
with an empty sack.

The hay in the loft
misses the night sky,
so the old roof
leaks a few stars.

Rain clouds gone,
and muddy paw prints
on the moon.

I've never learned from experience.
What else is there? you ask.
How about ninety billion galaxies.

What is it the wind has lost
that she keeps looking for
under each leaf?

I grow older.
I still like women, but mostly
I like Mexican food.

Sleeping on my right side I think
of God. On my left side, sex.
On my back I snore with my dog.

Some nights are three nights long,
some days a mere noon hour, then whistled
back to work, the heart dredging sludge.

The nightmare we waken from,
grateful, is somebody else's life.

Mirrors have always given the wrong
impression of me. So do other people.
So do I. Let's stop this right now.

The face you look out of
is never the face
your lover looks into.

The crumpled candy wrapper
is just another flower
to the rain.

How can I disappoint myself?
How many are within this brown
and wrinkled skin? Just one in pieces.

The stones turn their backs to us.
Our lives are light as flyspecks.

What has become
of the great hunter?
Today he won't kill flies.

Out in a field, an immense empty
pasture, clouds of leaves fell
from no visible trees. I was scared.

God's hand is cupped
over the crickety heart
of the turtle.

At the cabin I left the canola bottle open
and eleven mice drowned in this oil bath.
I had invented the mouse atom bomb.

The firefly's one word:
darkness!

A bumblebee,
a straggly rosebush
staining the air with her scent.
A blue and black butterfly —
too many Bs but life is like that.

How tall would I be
without my enemies
to measure me?

One grows tired of the hoax of up
and down. Jesus descended into a universe
of neither perfect lines, squares, nor circles.

You step in the same river once only
for an instant. Panhandle time with
the bruised fingers of what might have been.

"Charred beyond recognition" is bad news.
Yet it happens to us all. Ashes
have never returned to wood.

In an egg yolk,
an artery fine as the touch
of a feather.

The cowdogs caught their first jackrabbit.
Ace, the big male, is curled in the dirt
growling to protect his trophy, the bloody ears.

First deerfly emerged solstice morning
bent on hell, creature torture. But like Bush
among his fly friends he's a nice guy.

How lucky in one life to see
the sun lift a cloud from a pool!

This slender blue thread,
if anything,
connects everything.

The ninth time I screwed Ophelia
in a row I was still a garden hose
but then I woke up in Nebraska.

The Great Gourmand rows his boat
all day on a peanut butter sandwich
and warm water.

At my age,
even in airports,
why would you wish
time to move faster?

The clock stopped at 5:30 for three months.
Now it's always time to quit work,
have a drink, cook dinner.

The butterfly
jots a note on the wind
to remind itself of something.

How can it be
that everyone my age
is older than I?

Twisted my ankle
until it's blue.
Now I can feel my heart
beating in my foot.

How attentive the big bear resting his chin
on the bird feeder, an eye rolling toward my window
to see if he has permission for sunflower seeds.

On my desk two
indisputably great creations:
duct tape and saltine crackers.

The red-naped sapsucker
doesn't know its name is silly.
Oh you white guys, again.

In a pasture, wild turkeys
flip cow pies, looking for bugs.

Suddenly my clocks agree.
One has been stopped for several
months, but twice a day
they have this tender moment.

In deer season,
walking in the woods,
I sing like Pavarotti.

"What I would do for wisdom,"
I cried out as a young man.
Evidently not much. Or so it seems.
Even on walks I follow the dog.

The owl is a bronze urn of ashes
till one of the round seals blinks.

Crow with a red beak
looks over his shoulder.

After rowing my blue and brown boat
for three hours I liked the world again,
the two loons close by, the theory of red wine.

Waited all day for the moon to rise.
It just happened.
I can't believe my luck.

I saw a black butterfly
as big as a raven
flapping through the night.
Maybe it was an owl.

Ten mousetraps in the cellar
and one dead mouse.
Pretty good odds for living.

In 1947 a single gold nugget was found
hereabouts. Old men still look for a second one.
In between life has passed.

In my garden
the late sun glows
through a rabbit's ears.

Midday silence is different
from nighttime silence.
I can't tell you how.

Between the four pads
of a dog's foot,
the fragrance of grass.

July, and fat black flies
so slow you can bat them
right out of the air.

Dead raccoon, legs in the air,
washes his paws in the sky.

Flecks of foam
on the fountain's lips
as it reads aloud from
the scripture of water.

This morning,
fish bleed into nacreous clouds
and an iron bird walks to town
on the bottom of the river.

I'm so pleased that Yeats
never got off his stilts
though I have only one.

I have used up more than
20,000 days waiting to see
what the next would bring.

It's hard to believe there's a skeleton
inside us, not certainly in the beautiful
girl getting out of her red car.

Elaborate is the courtliness
of the imagination, on one sore knee
before beauty.

When I touched her long feet
I stopped walking.
When I tasted her mouth
I quit eating.

When I watched her hands
as she peeled a potato,
I gave up everything I owned.

I have grown old, and know
how an owl feels,
seeing a man with a lantern.

November cold. Hey, grasshopper!
What goes? Once all that armor
weighed nothing!

In winter, don't ever
touch your tongue
to someone cold.

Fresh snow standing deep
on the phone wire. If you call me,
speak softly.

Well before dawn I woke
up crying because my teeth hurt.
Lucky for me there was soothing rain
on the cabin roof.

I woke up as nothing. Now start piling
it on. No. Yes. No. Maybe. Indoors.
Outdoors. Me. You. Her corpse said stop.

Birds and bugs
flying left and right.
Always the question,
What to do next?

The wasp
has built his palace
in a bell.

Life has always yelled at me,
"Get your work done." At least
that's what I think she says.

The patience of the spider's web
is not disturbed by dew.

Time makes us supplicant whores.
Ray Carver told me he was missing years.
The bottle's iron mouth suckles the brain dry.

The old Finn (85) walks
twenty-five miles to see his brother.
Why? "I don't have no car."

Look again: that's not
a yellow oak leaf on the path,
but the breastplate from a turtle.

The robins are back,
so weary from flying that they walk
wherever they go.

When we were young we talked
about bottomless lakes, which meant to us
the same lakes were bottomless in China.

You had to milk the cows at 5 A.M.
and 5 P.M. or they'd start bawling.
Even udders can become brutal clocks.

That winter the night fell seven
times a day and horses learned
to run under the ground.

Time flew in and out of the window
until she dropped dead in the kitchen.

At the end, just a pinch of the world
is all we have left to hold on to,
the hem of a sheet.

What if everyone you've loved
were still alive? That's the province
of the young, who don't know it.

A new spring and it's still 5:30
on the cabin's clock. It's always dawn
or time for dinner. My favorites.

If a camel can stretch its muzzle
out of its own stink
so can I.

Lazed on the floor like an old baby
for three hours, then rowed my blue
and brown boat.

Oh, to be in love,
with all five buckets
of the senses
overflowing!

On the shoulder, the turtle
warily holds out his head
on the end of a stick.

The moon, all lordly white,
an anti-rose embedded
at dawn in a thin veil
of red clouds.

Their balls were so swollen they collided
their motorcycles at 70 mph
with only momentary regret.

It's nice to think that when
we're fossils we'll all be in the same
thin layer of rock.

Oh, to write just one poem
that would last as long as that rose
tattooed on her butt!

The imagination's kisses
are a cloud of butterflies.

We should
sit like a cat
and wait for the door
to open.

In our farthest field,
between one walk
and the next,
the arrival of ten billion
grasshoppers.

How sharp must be the fletcher's knife
to split a feather
and leave in both halves flight.

The old hen scratches
then looks, scratches then looks.
My life.

Every time I've had a sea change
I thought I was dying.
I probably was.

My stopped clock is always
jumping ahead,
a sure winner in the race with time,
with every day as long as I wish it to be.

A vermilion flycatcher flew too far north
and died in Montana. The same for a Michigan wolf
in Missouri. I get butchered in New York
but don't mind it. I rise again the third day.

Bucket in the rain,
rejoice!

Deerflies die by the billions, the cool air
so clear you drink it in gulps
and the moon drifts closer to the cabin door.

Sometimes fate will steal a baby
and leave an old man
soft as a bundle of rags.

So happy with my fat old body,
still quick enough to slap a fly.

Black dog on white snow
beside the flooding, brown river.
This is where I live!

I feel
the bear's heart
in her footprints.

To have reverence for life
you must have reverence for death.
The dogs we love are not taken from us
but leave when summoned by the gods.

You asked, *What makes you sure?*
I have the faith of the blind,
I answered.

Wish-wash. Ten thousand tons of peanuts
free to us monkeys for 10,000 years.
Oh taste and see, but not in a hurry.

One barred owl harried by
eight loud crows.
A thief besieged by thieves.

A light snow shows
that even the old wagon track
is new.

I hope there's time
for this and that,
and not just this.

Pout and drift. The poet self-sunk
for three months looks up at the dark
heavens, puzzled by moon and stars.

The butterfly's brain,
the size of a grain of salt,
guides her to Mexico.

Buddhists say everything is led by mind.
My doubts are healed by drinking
a bottle of red wine in thirty-three minutes.

DNA shows that I'm the Unknown Soldier.
I can't hear the birds down here,
only politicians shitting out of their mouths.

The water spider
bounces on his legs
but cannot shake the lake.

The low ceiling grazes
the tops of the tall pines
encircling the yard.
Even the air feels crushed.

Peach sky
at sunset,
then (for god's sake)
one leaf across
the big October moon.

Dust too
is drawn on wings
to light.

Last year the snake
left her skin on the floor,
diaphanous like the name
of a lovely girl you've forgotten —
but not her flesh.

I'm sixty-two and can drop dead
at any moment. Thinking this in August
I kissed the river's cold moving lips.

The colder the raindrops
the harder they knock
on the door.

Come to think of it,
there's no reason to decide
who you are.

Stars from horizon to horizon.
A whole half universe
just to light the path.

Rilke says the new year brings things that have
never been, forgetting "won't be again."
Even a dog is never lost in the same place.

Awake in Paris all night listening to rain.
It's lucky there's nothing to eat, a fat dog
waiting for the luck of a roadkill possum.

I prefer the skyline
of a shelf of books.

Imagine a gallery
where all the paintings
opened and closed their wings!

In Brazil I leapt
out of my skin, then back
into it, a onetime-only trick.

Sometimes all it takes
to be happy
is a dime on the sidewalk.

When women pleasure themselves, I heard
at age twelve, they tweak their left ear
then move on to greatness.

Her voice had a deep resonance
that must have made her pubic hair
buzz.

The moon put her hand
over my mouth and told me
to shut up and watch.

I surely understand paper and how poets
disappear despite it. These days I write
so lightly I don't quite touch it.

A man pays court with his poems.
A woman dismisses him with hers.

Monkeys search each other
and so do we. Another sign
of our advancement.

All those spin butchers drooling
public pus. Save your first
bullet for television.

Rate the hours. One and 5 A.M.
are fine while 3 is the harshest.
The fool always feels safe at noon.

I thought my friend was drinking
too much, but it was the vodka
that was drinking him.

An uncommon number of us die
on our birthdays. You turn a bend
and abruptly you're back home.

Now that I'm older I perfectly
recall the elephant's eye
and the whale's eye that blinked.

That little red eye behind the toilet?
And we think poets
have a baleful look.

This is the county fair
and everything has a bull's ring
through its nose.
Who is leading?

After fifty years of tracking clouds
I've become cold rain upon my life.
How odd to see the mist so clearly.

Autumn dusk, and in the grass
the spiders' gray funnels
drain off the light.

In the electric chair's harness,
one man hauls all the darkness.

Our lives as highlights on TV:
our best lays and meals,
our backward flights of drunken
fancy down the stairs.

These house-trailer fires kill thousands
who will no longer suffer
the opinions and scorn of the rich.

Coming home from the tavern—
I see the pile of dirty clothes
on the cabin floor move.
Doglike, the snake is getting comfortable.

The path disappeared. There was a field
with no edges over which I walked
through the sky which blanketed the ground.

In this lowbrow wilderness
in the area of the black-phase wolf,
I give up my opinions.

A house will turn itself
to catch a little moonlight
on a bedpost.

It's the Devil's
blessing
that flies sleep
at night.

In the house the lizard's enemy
is porcelain. They struggle in the sink.
Warren, the cat, finds them there.

The tree also died the exact
moment the old raven fell off
a lower branch.

A frosty morning,
and one mosquito
at rest on the lip
of the tub.

Sometimes the teakettle rattles
over the flame with the *And! And! And!*
of a child telling a story too big
to pour out all at once.

So the Greeks had amphorae
with friezes of nymphs.
We have coffee mugs with ads
for farm equipment!

How evil all priesthoods.
All over the earth Holy Places
soaked with extra blood.

The handle of its neck
clucks back and forth
and ratchets the turkey
forward.

How is it the rich always know
what is best for the poor?

Trelawny burned Shelley's heart
while thousands of poets
were waiting for transplants.

Lush petals
and glistening thorns —
this college
full of experts.

The poet holds the podium
in both hands
like a garbage bag of words.

See how the rich and famous
sniff the tips of their fingers.
What have they been touching?

Ikkyū was awakened by a crow's caw,
which is not the same as an alarm clock.
He adored the whore dressed in gold brocade.
O master, why count flowers that are gone?

On the nightstand,
a copy of *Prevention* magazine
and the night coming on.

Like an old dog
I slowly lower and arrange myself
in a heap of sighs.

Scientists say the moon grows 1½ inches
farther away every year. I'll fight
this cosmic terrorism hand to hand.

What I learned: Dogs walk upstairs
for nothing. Don't eat with your nose.
Tonight the moon owns this river.

Often I travel at night and am surprised
where I end up at dawn. All road signs and maps
are hoaxes. Don't forget the earth is round.

Earth touched Moon
with his shadow, and Moon
blushed. Everyone saw it.

"When the roll is called up yonder
I'll be there," they sang. Hopefully.
Maybe. But maybe not.

Foolish me,
to think my wine
would never turn.

Come close to death
and you begin to see
what's under your nose.

On the cabin floor a trapped mouse
covers maggots that writhe.
With this in sight,
allow me to squeak.

I've been married since birth.
All other women sense the bottomless
depth of my insincerity.

She owns a perfect butt
but her loutish husband calls
it his "reserved seat."

Without her scarves
the weeping willow
has a twisted body.

They're putting a new green tin roof
on my moss-covered cabin.
Bang, what violence.

It rained so hard the sky became water
and under a mantle of trees I gulped for air.
Here on the bottom the water rose to my chin,
and my face ached to grow gills.

A welcome mat of moonlight
on the floor. Wipe your feet
before getting into bed.

Bullfrog groans.
He is the wooden floor
under the cold feet of the night.

The full moon often rises
in the wrong place. Tonight I sense
activity up there, a general unrest.

My wife's lovely dog, Mary, kills
butterflies. They're easier than birds.
I wonder if Buddha had dog nature.

Three teeth pulled including
a prime buck. Tongue probes
the jaw's lonesome holes.

Alone in the car
we try to tell ourselves
some good news.

These headlights
swim right through
the seine of falling snow.

In our October windfall time red
apples on frostbitten green grass.
You learn to eat around the wormholes.

As long as the woodpecker
taps on my roof I'll be fine,
a little life left in the shell.

The blind man navigates
by stars behind the daylight.

Just before I fly out of myself
I'll say a puzzled goodbye.
Our bodies are women who were never
meant to be faithful to us.

I was born a baby.
What has been
added?

Treasure what you find
already in your pocket, friend.

Today a pink rose in a vase
on the table.
Tomorrow, petals.

The pastures grow up
with red cedars
once the horses are gone.

About the Poets

Ted Kooser and Jim Harrison live in Nebraska, Montana, Michigan, and on the U.S.–Mexico border. This book is a rather avian triangulation of their brotherhood.

The Chinese character for poetry is made up of two parts: "word" and "temple." It also serves as pressmark for Copper Canyon Press. Founded in 1972, Copper Canyon Press remains dedicated to publishing poetry exclusively, from Nobel laureates to new and emerging authors. The Press thrives with the generous patronage of readers, writers, booksellers, librarians, teachers, students, and funders — everyone who shares the conviction that poetry invigorates the language and sharpens our appreciation of the world.

PUBLISHERS' CIRCLE

The Allen Foundation for the Arts
Lannan Foundation
National Endowment for the Arts

EDITORS' CIRCLE

Thatcher Bailey
The Breneman Jaech Foundation
Cynthia Hartwig and Tom Booster
Target Stores
Emily Warn and Daj Oberg
Washington State Arts Commission

CONTRIBUTING EDITORS' CIRCLE

Bruce S. Kahn and Karen G. Hufnagle

For information and catalogs:

COPPER CANYON PRESS
Post Office Box 271
Port Townsend, Washington 98368
360/385-4925
www.coppercanyonpress.org

This book is set in Adobe Jensen. Jensen is a digital reflection
of typefaces designed in fifteenth-century Venice. Book interior
design and composition by Valerie Brewster, Scribe Typography.
Printed on archival-quality Glatfelter Author's Text
at McNaughton & Gunn, Inc.

Braided Creek is also issued in a signed, limited edition
of 250 numbered copies. An additional twenty-six copies have
been lettered *A* to *Z* with holograph poems by each poet.